WHISPERING LEAVES

THE RUSTLE

LALITA VAITHEESWARAN

This book is dedicated to the loving memories of my father who is in our hearts forever.

When I was a child,

You always held my hand.

With immense gratitude,teary eyes I stand.

You lived a plain life to paint mine with sparkling hue

In every life dear appa,I'd only want you.

Contents

Contents

Contents

Contents

Contents

Acknowledgements

I'm Indebted to my family who has been my support at every step of my venture.

My immense gratitude to the Almighty for His benevolence showered on us.

Thank you ***Notion Press*** for this publication.

Cover page and other images courtesy : ***Unsplash.com***

Preface

The poems in this book depict a downpour of an emotional cascade of sorts. They evoke multiple fervors and sentiments. They are of various genres portraying the diverse images of our society compelling us to introspect and make the world a better place to live in.

The last section of the book has a few poems in the *invented verse form* which are different from the traditional forms.

Almost every poem has been honored with an award of excellence or appreciation by various literary platforms.

1. Chime in rhyme

As the morning temple chimed ding-dong

The schools announced they're starting, with the gong

The goat in the pastures shook their bells to tinkle

The elephant running amok, made its fetters jingle!

The metal gates of the church opened and shut with a clang

The soprano of the choir reverberated as the inmates sang

The belfry on the façade with the small carillons ringing

The magical enchanted ether reverberates in singing

While it echoes through misty air, it's the resounding of the peal

The city clocks tintinnabulating, adding to the festive zeal

The green fields have the oxen ploughing with a jangle

The warbling stream are hushing the cows as they amble

The cymbals and the tambourines add to the rattle

As the sun sets and brings back home the cattle

Every element of nature creates divine music and chime

While the poet interlaces alliteration in poetry to rhyme!

2. Rain

As they hugged and huddled with each other
The ball of clouds meandered and wandered
The sky turned violet as it shivered and quivered
To the evil, grey clouds rumbling in thunder
A dazzling sparkle lit up the somber, subdued vault
The rumble changed into an angry growling roar
The trees stooped and swayed to murmur and whisper
Their inability to handle the ongoing tantrums anymore
Tiny droplets as pure crystals cascaded to the earth's bosom
Quenching the thirst of the dreary, barren, arid terrain
Drenched with the angelic drizzle inundating my soul
I felt my negativity washing out with the welcome rain!
Flooding and submerging the unwelcome bygones of the past
Downpour, as it metamorphosed into a torrential deluge
It splashed and cleansed the pneuma of every being
Under its gracious benevolence, my imprisoned mind found refuge.

3. Character

He was essaying the role of the villain
Wherein he had to hit, badger and slay
He was hated by every audience that watched
Evoking anger on his shades of grey!

His lips muttered foul language; his actions violence showered
He looked repulsive and hideous on the screen
Every evil he could carry out with ease
Cruelest of the cruel, meanest of the mean!
The hero, on the other hand was an epitome of goodness
Oh! how he would bring in a fresh breeze of glee
The audience would love, worship and adore him
And all his plays, they would rush to see
Once in the town there came a bad spell
People starved as famine and drought hit
The villain was seen distributing his wealth
While the hero hoarded and in his comfort sit!
The people were flabbergasted at this change
They set out amazed to reasons seek and hunt
The Villain laughed saying it was only a "character" he played
While in real life he was a saintly man full of stunt!
The hero was a miser full of intentions bad
He had cheated, lied and thrived on others' misery
These are the reel characters who influence our real lives

And we fall into their trap ...that's the irony!

4

4. The sinking ship -A doctor's life

As she lay in the hospital bed, tied to tubes
Breathing hard to keep herself alive
It was imperative, she had caught the disease
As in the ocean of the pandemic she had dived
Every moment, every hour as she had catered to them
Giving them hope, optimism and good will
Her loved ones she had been forced to forsake
Towards saving humanity diverting her every skill
With no sleep or rest or food for her needs
Bound to her duties she stayed awake
In the midst of the raging chaos that ensued
Her own medicines she forgot to take
As her sinking ship with helplessness stares
Looking for an anchor adrift the life's ocean
She continues to be the inspirational ship's hull
How I wish there was a magical potion!

5. Prayer in poetry

Exaltation of the higher self was discovered

Through poetry as it created verses pure as a stream

The depressed found peace and solace when they read

As they turned their hopes to the divine supreme!

Words served as the straw to hold on

In times of melancholy, gloom and despair

In times when people lived for hatred and in fear

Poetic words were heavenly and blissful like the prayer

Poems are not mere words that rhyme

But carry the essence of atonement true

The words which have wronged can now be made right

The poetic flow makes man turn over a leaf new

Just as we surrender ourselves to God through words

Poetry has the power of goodness and penance,

A healing touch, a mystical cure through words

Prayer and poetry are the spectrum of the same reverence.

6. A walk to remember

Tied to narrow minded prejudiced patriarchs

In handcuffs and shackles, I walked through dingy lanes

Caged, imprisoned, my wings were clipped

My dreams were shattered to fragmented remains

I was blindfolded by strong iron hands which hurt

As I was pushed and shoved into the realms of despair

Trampled and tortured into yielding to their will

Threatening into destruction and decimation if I dared

The onlookers sighed and helplessly watched

The cavalcade of tyranny pompously spanned with rejoice

Compelling, constraining, choking my free will

Overpowering and smothering every revolting meek voice

Through the gossamer armor that covered my eyes

I perceived a bright light at the end of the track narrow

Wisdom and knowledge set forth its divine tentacles

Encouraging me to traverse the fearless path from tomorrow

Suddenly I felt a surge of strength, intense and strong from within

I overpowered and conquered those to whom my soul had surrendered

Slain and slaughtered, their ego and ignorance fell, defeated and shamed

Triumphing over captivity, I walked free…a walk that I shall forever

remember!

7. Genetics of English

Strands of chromatin wrapped as words

Embedded on them the twenty six genes

Mutating as different parts of speech

The most powerful a communication means

Vowels and consonants the genetic make up determine

A missing gene can give the meaning a difference

Every gene has an allocated defined place

An extra one can change the word essence

A string of pearls which the dictionary make

Alleles created with silent sounds as in "know" and "knife"

Phenotypically 'two', 'to' and 'too' look the same

But genotypically a barrage of difference endow!

Oh dear, the twenty six genes, the alphabet!

The world would have been silent without you!

Your dominant traits uphold the language

You carry the DNA of English true!

8. Breathe in experience, breathe out poetry

Every occasion, every event

As it etched on the soul

Many merriments gave

While others on lives, took a heavy toll

Some remained as scars

Scathing the psyche each day

While others gave the impetus to live

Keeping fears at bay

Emotional outbursts of angst

Distress, anguish, anger or agony

Found their place as ink flowing on paper

As catharsis to many

The joyful moments of triumph

Exuberance and jubilation

Danced through poetic expressions

To celebrate till its culmination

As love and passion blossomed

Words through symphonies danced

Becoming messengers of warmth

flaming the emotions of romance

Incidents gave words a wand

To shape their magical wonder

Poetry was born out of
Experience in opulent splendor!

9. Emancipation

Caged in the prison of flesh and bone
Imprisoned for years to suffer alone
Shackled by materialistic goals to achieve
Some virtues to be proud, some vices to grieve
The subtleness of the ego which perches atop
The avarice and desires that never cease to stop
At last, culminate with the mortal remains
Leaving behind all material losses and gains!
The soul breathes for a while; unbound and free
It chirps and twitters like the flying birds in glee
Carrying with it the impressions of the subtle body last
To get implanted into a new form of life, in a new body, fast
Alas! it is liberated, a new era, another to delve upon
With the karma of the previous birth, the same soul is reborn!
While the new body in its new form cries in delight
The soul gets from the old lock-up some respite!
When the good karma exceeds, the soul reaches its destination!
***Atman** meeting **Parmatman**; the soul attains emancipation!*
Glossary
Atman = Soul
Parmatman = The Supreme Being

10. Illusion

The little boy thought he could see ghosts
In the night as the trees swayed
Eerie shadows which moved back and forth
Hide and seek, the dark silhouettes played!
News spread far and wide in to the people around
Who looked for means to scare the ghosts away
Rituals and prayers, black-magic and sorcery
Every means to douse and keep peoples' fears at bay
The people were asked to give their recounts
At different times of the night and day
Some were too scared to face the ordeal
While others a brave and valiant face display!
"Yes! It's a black creature and its eyes shine"
Said another," Its moves like a cloud going astray"
"It makes swooshing sounds, whistles and hoots"
"And when we try to touch it, there's a misty spray'
At last, the wise old man stepped in
And proved his mettle and his wisdom of his greys
The shadow of the trees, the hooting of the owl and the drizzle
Created a scary illusion of imaginary portray!

11. The prism rainbow

On the canvas of my life, splattered with elan

Were the colors black and grey, which ubiquitously ran

Depression and melancholy scattered dullness and gloom

Desolate feelings sprung from the fear of death and doom

As the morning ball of gold spread its yellow golden rays

Enthusiasm, optimism and happiness began making its way

A little birdie chirped and sang and brought in some cheer of blue

My tumultuous stormy mind began a journey of calmness new

The greenery of nature fluttered to shed some of her hue in resplendence

Harmonious melodies brought forth vitality and prosperity in abundance

The Lavender, Iris, Lilac and Bellflower, when purple tint in the fragrant air splash

Divinity and spiritual knowledge imbued in my inner self as a mystical flash

As the sun set and turned the azure sky into a crimson vault livid

A turbulence of power, energy, passion and desires began their display vivid

I collected these shades in my lacy white strings of the heart's harmony

Tatting them into tassels of purity, innocence and virtuous symphony

I found myself singing the motley, variegated, songs of the rainbow

As the myriad of colors assorting orange and embracing the indigo!

12. Ambition

The desire to achieve, as it reached its zenith
Every means employed was brought into play
By hook or by crook the conscience was thrown
For the desirous determination to find its way.
The stairs to success were jumped in a hurry
Trampling innocent onlookers who viewed in dismay
Thousands of hearts were trodden, lakhs were destroyed
Survival of the fittest found predators and its prey!
The pinnacle was reached, as resolute it was, as a rock
The cost of the desire could not match up to the harm that lay
The loss had been heavy in emotions and wrecking relationships
Not even the value of zilch the acquired achievement could weigh!
Yes, ambitions should drive every being's dreary life
But a line drawn to keep awry and skewed desires away
Let the mind ruminate and set the goals to a purer self
Live and let live should be the only ambition everyday!

13. Strangers on a journey

As I took a shared cab, it was already midnight
My odd working hours usually put me in this plight
The roads were deserted; only flood lights were showing the way
Crossing my fingers, with a thumping heart, my lips began to pray
Suddenly at the turning, a stranger hitched, to get into the car
He had a bag, a book in his hand, and on his shoulders was a guitar!
Tall and thin with affable looks, he settled on the seat next to me
Striking a light conversation, he was trying to be friendly
He talked about the clouds, the sky and the fathomless sea
After a reticent start, I found myself talking to him happily!
It was a while, and as we reached our destination,
I looked sideways, shockingly to find that there was no one
I asked the driver where did my co-passenger disappear?
Surprised, the driver exclaimed "who? There was but no one here."

14. Market

I was a shopaholic, going on a shopping spree
Every article bought, filled me with glee !
I had a cupboard, overflowing with dresses new
But whenever there was an occasion, I always thought I had very few
So again, I went on to buy some more
Dresses, shoes, cosmetics, accessories galore
A hoarder at heart, I had a huge collection of some kind
I had every design, every variety -you name it and you'll find!
A time then came, when you couldn't, step out of home
There was no place to flaunt your dress, no where you could roam
There was no need to have more than a decent pair
There was no event to showcase your fashion-wear!
As my possessions lay unused, the gap between greed and need was in sight
I learnt the lesson of minimalism, and that it's wise to travel light !

15. You me and tea

16. Butterfly

Motley iridescent wings fluttering high in the sky
Like aromatic flowers in spring, flying high
Celestial ambrosia she collects radiating her hue
The blooms and the blossoms nestle her essence new
Not long ago she was an ugly caterpillar which crawled
Then a brown pupa which lazed cocooned and hauled
She was dejected and depressed by her ugly appearance
Wanting to end her life for this disgraceful, unsightly presence
Her inner voice asked her to perseverance and patience keep
To wait with fortitude to show her inner beauty deep
The inconsolable indolent part began to show a change gradual
Out came a pair of vivid, intense wings, glowing and beautiful!
The success looking beautiful is not quickly got! sigh!
Many changes convert a caterpillar into a beautiful butterfly!

17. Hope

Let's all hope for a sunny tomorrow
The sun shall spread its golden rays
There would be only joy and no sorrow!
Yes! There shall be again those beautiful days
We would sing in glee and laugh in cheer
The sun shall spread its golden rays!
The rainbows and blossoming flowers shall reappear
The stars adorning the angelic vault blue
We would sing in glee and laugh in cheer!
Days would clothe in blissful gaiety new
Perfumed breeze pervading the air
The stars adorning the angelic vault blue!
Melodies and harmonies would echo everywhere
Vibrant hues, motley flowers spread
Perfumed breeze pervading the air!
There would be no more fear or dread
No melancholy; only joys in oro
Vibrant hues, motley flowers spread
There would be only joy and no sorrow!

18. Road to success

The roads were difficult, arduous and grueling
Tempting me to quit them all
There were deep gorges and ravines beneath them
One wrong step, and I would fall!
As I walked in continuous, incessant steps
The destination was clear in my mind
I focused my vision rivetted to the future
Leaving all my fears and insecurities behind!
I stumbled and fell many times in a day
Getting up exhausted, weary and ready to retreat
Giving up on the very goals that I lived for
I agreed to accept my own defeat!

My ambition and determination to be a go getter
Pushed me again to resume my journey to seek
Shunning any slack negligent attitude to overpower me
I reassured myself I was strong and not weak !

The roads ultimately narrowed in on a lane
Where everything was approachable and in easy access
I realized I had reached my coveted destination
I had chosen my path to success

19. A special gift

The box was beautifully wrapped
Tied all around with ornate ribbons blue
The wrapping paper glittered and gleamed
Reflecting and reverberating with vibrant hue
With a thumping heart that raced with joy
Her anklets tinkled into a merry sound
She wondered what could be inside the box
"Could it be what I wanted?' She thought aloud!
As she unboxed the attractive gift
Out came with loud cheer and delight
Her freedom to choose, her period of emancipation
Her decision to opt, and exercise her right!
She could now voice her opinions, take decisions,
She had now the right to say a big NO!
There was no vulnerability for her being the fairer sex
Her life was filled with happiness throwing out the woes!

The liberated woman of today got a gift special
Her freedom that was being throttled by some
Was trampled and crushed to set her free
A liberated soul she had now become!

20. The garden of Eden

A perfect paradise, pure and pristine
Where there'd be no sorrows but only pleasure
Let's build it again with our love
A garden of ecstasy and bliss beyond measure!
Every intent pure and untainted
No hatred, no temptations to err or sin
No evil in the garb of the satan
Only the voice of conscience from within!
The perfect symphony of the man and the woman
For lures, guilt or shame there remains no place
Let's build it with joy, rapture and beatitude
A garden of contentment, and Heavenly grace
Every heart overpowered with love and peace
Where every mind only positivity emanates
A garden with humans who wouldn't now stumble
And make this world where only goodness originates!

21. Balloons

Tattered and torn, the little boy was clad
Selling balloons to children, he saw them going glad
Papa! mumma! I want some more!
Red, blue and green there are colors galore
The balloon seller was happier, as he would earn more
He limped on his bare feet which had gone sore
To children, some dreams of the heavens afar as he sold
Gleeful, exuberant, sanguine sounds of children rolled
He had never lived upon the fairy world enchanting
No one to buy him balloons as he's on his toes panting
The balloons to one are an enthralling world of childhood
The balloons to the other are painful means of livelihood

22. Burning desires

When desires enflamed the interstices of the heart
The mind a futile elusive shadow chase
What was desirous to the heart was averse to the intellect
As wants and duties interlaced in a maze
The lines between the pining and the onuses
Thinned and faded as the heart conquered the clique
Wicked wants and longings for the vices grew stronger
The powerful trampled and crushed the meek!
Flames of passion rose to violate the weaker sex
As impulses and hankerings lost their grip going wild
Freedom to crave went berserk and uninhibited
Rules and laws were broken; every purity defiled
Let there be desires burning for good virtues
Let happiness, equality, justice and truth invade in magnanimity
Let the world be a better place to live in
Let's all pledge to uphold this overwhelming action in unanimity!

23. The cage (Limericks)

There was this big cage of iron

Where the circus had kept a ferocious lion

It roared vehemently all day

Keeping visitors at bay

It was the popular spectacle's doyen

There were other animals too

Who were kept caged in the zoo

They all belonged to the same circus

And were accused of creating a ruckus

So were being punished for the hullabaloo

At night when the curator went near

Thinking of those wild animals, shivering in fear

He started laughing, guffawing, howling aloud

The sky was now clear of the grey cloud

As the "animals" were actually humans in animal wear!

24. Two square meals

The hustle bustle, the push and pull
Their day transforms from a sleeping lull
Toiling hard, working full of zeal
To earn their two square meals!
Heavy rain or snow or scorching heat
They are always at their two feet
Their poverty only their Achilles heel!
They are out to labour for their two square meals!
Live and let live is their only cry
Give me work and don't let me die
I need to survive and tis an appeal!
Please let me have my two square meals!

25. Footprints of the conscience

On the sands of time your footprints were found
Over the years when I thought I'd lost you
The paths you tread, well defined as I looked
Leading to the destined glorious purposeful stop
As I followed, shadowing them step by step,
Curvy and tortuous were the roads you took
Arduous, onerous journey of the soul
It wasn't simple, straightforward a voyage
Tedious, overbearing as my esse' started to crumble
I held on to the shadows trailing to reach the truth
Wherein at last I reached my destination.

26. The golden moment

I waited in patience, for the moment of zenith, in my life

That golden moment, which would free me, of my turbulent strife

Every day, I would look afar to see whether it's on the way

Lazing, lying on the couch, waiting for it the whole day!

With keen ears on the door, eyes wide open to seize

The one glorious instant to put the whole life at ease

There was a knock at my door, and in came an opportunity new

I overlooked it with disdainful derision, and bid it a contemptuous adieu!

Such many chances looking meek, kissed my feet off and on

But my wait for that golden moment, allowed them to slip with scorn

*At last, one night, **The God of Opportunity, Tyche,** appeared in my dreams*

He said, "You do not want your golden moment of fame it seems!"

"Of course", said I "I have been waiting for that special time"

He laughed "every opportunity that you threw was a golden moment sublime"

Every small and big event can be made golden by only you

It's our choice and perception of a moment, the way we view!

27. Autumn leaves

As Autumn makes the leaves fall down
Taking leave from their abode so dear
Paying magical colorful tributes to the ground
Letting go of the past they, have no sorrow but cheer
They symbolize to the world a cycle of life
From green to brown as they their attire change
How every living being is brought to dust
Decoding the eternal truth that looks strange
New leaves would now sprout as the old give way
Glittery with the ambrosia of the sparkling dew
Autumn leaves rustle and whistle as they cling tight
Only to disembark and enter into a novel world of another hue
Brilliantly colored leaves fall to depict winter's melancholy
Teaching courage, and adapting to change, in every sphere
Though the joys and prosperity of spring are short lived
An enchanted season of souls is here!

28. First day of the woman

The woman after confinement when becomes a mother
Delivering a daughter, on her first day, she shudders!
As the girl is born amongst grief and rejoice
The first day turns out a necessity and not a choice!
The first day the small girl child wants to go to school
Her books are dropped and she is shown the rule
The first day when the charming angel's dress stains red,
She becomes an untouchable, impure fiend instead!
Her first day in the workplace turns an ogling day
A free show for lechers while she watches all in dismay!
Her first day of seeking matrimony becomes a trade
When for meeting demands, relationships are made!
Life throws on her, disgrace, dishonor on her first fall
Every first occasion turns a misfortune and a calamity befalls

29. Teachers Day

You taught me to read, you taught me to write
You helped me reach soaring heights
You gave me the impetus in life to achieve my goals
To mold me into what I am, you had the prime role
Right from the wrong I learnt how to discern
In this unscrupulous world, a good name to earn
Wisdom and knowledge you poured on me in abundance
In the guise of sternness, pouring your love in resplendence
Oh, dear teachers! humbled, I stand in gratitude today!
From darkness towards light, you tirelessly lead the way

30. The doorbell

When the milkman rings the doorbell,
Its the break of a new morn
The morning basket bringing bread and cereals
Tells us that the day is born!
Then comes the maid ringing it again
Oh how I run to open in glee!
Thanking my stars that she has arrived
How happy a sight that is to see!
The delivery boys ring the doorbell
Bringing in vegetables and grocery
A marvel that service is at the doorstep
Its innumerable times things they ferry!
Afternoon doorbells are the most exciting
As there is the mail-man or a parcel arrived
How, despite these severe harsh days of the pandemic,
These helpers made us survive!
There were old days when the doorbells
Irritated and always disturbed me
But now every door bell that comes
Makes me realise that its a blessing to just be !

31. Down memory lane: The tears of a mother

As I sat on the reclining chair

Desolate, deserted in the old age home

To the old days of glory and happiness

My memories meandered and roamed!

Marriage and children made me complete

As I held my toddlers close to my bosom each day

Every moment of my life I dedicated for their rearing up

Dancing to their tunes as they say!

Holding their hands, I taught them things new

Their every tantrum I tolerated with spirits high

Sleepless nights in their sickness I suffered

Their slightest worries would make me cry

As they grew up they chose their lives own

While I grew older and of use no more

The children began to shift me to each other

I was one after the other shown doors

Today as I sit in melancholy and gloom

Desperate for the touch of a loving hand

I hold on to the happy memories of the yore

To survive as I cling to them strand by strand

32. The gypsy soul

Like the free birds, I meander in the skies
Wandering like the ball of clouds which go by
Like raindrops trickling one by one
Like the golden rays emanating from the sun
I touch and kiss the mountain peaks high
Like the flakes of snow, in gay abandon I lie
Frolicking along the gardens of vivid hue
Fragrance of ethereal air, as I travel I imbue
I have no abode, liberated I roam
Making every loving heart my home
From the shackles of the world, I have set myself free
I am emancipated, I have the soul of a gypsy

33. Conversation with nature

As I watered my plants their leaves rustled in glee
The motley flowers swayed their heads in happiness
The breeze tugged and hugged me in delight
And in gratitude did my pneuma they caress
A small pearly dew winked as it sparkled
The cuckoo on the branches cocked its head to sing
The green grass nodded as it waved in harmony
A symphony was being born as rhapsody rang in
The azure sky was holding cotton balls in its bosom
Which like minstrels in gay abandon wandered
They signaled to me that it'd be a warm day
I looked up as the bright golden ball meandered
A drizzle appeared from nowhere clinging on my soul bare
Puzzled as I watched, the naughty duo to ask
Hey! a while ago you told me you'd not pour
And in the warmth of your cloak, I could bask?
They smiled and said they're playing hide-and-seek
The pond in the neighborhood wanted a splash
I pretended to be upset even while joyous within
My conversation with nature was nothing less than a bash!

34. Anklet

I look for you with a single anklet in hand
This one had dropped as you had walked on the shore
Mesmerised as I followed your steps
I was left asking for more!
You had turned back with a smile
And had beckoned me to follow you
I walked as if in a trance behind
The chiming and tinkling anklets were in view!
You took me to the secluded woods
Under the shady trees of May
I was lost in the enthralling aura
It was like a dream which had come to stay
I tried to touch you, to embrace and entwine
But you were elusive as a mystic illusion!
I have your anklet as a proof of your being
But were you for real or a magical deception?

35. Hemming

"Mother! my skirt is going into tatters
Stitch it all around it's gathers
I become the target of scornful attention
Our poverty is the burning issue of mention!"
"Give it to me", said the poor mother in great pain
As she threaded the needle with tremendous eye strain,
"The hemming would hold your attire for a while
Saving you from disgrace, and people wicked and guile"
The rich girl flaunted her new dress in stride
Asking the tailor to shorten it big and wide
"My short dress should grab all the attention,
And my beautiful figure getting all the mention
See that you hem it with thread sturdy and strong
As I display it to the town all day long!"
Hemming was done in both the dresses of the poor and the rich
For one it was a saving grace, for the other a display pitch!

36. The Banyan tree

The most revered of all the trees
Is the Vatvriksha or Banyan Tree
Symbolizing the universe,
It's the abode of the divine trinity
Granting fulfilment of worldly wishes
It's a shelter by God to His devotee
Its roots go down several feet
Called bahupada, they represent longevity
The magnificent benevolence of enormous magnitude,
It's is a sign of immortality
Renouncing the worldly pleasures, giving under its shade
Is the power of spirituality
*Associated with the **Lord of Death** Yama*
It also boasts of medicinal properties
Oh! Divine tree! we all pay our reverence to thee.

37. The next page

As the newborn was brought into this world

She cried and announced that she's here to stay

That she was no lesser than her counterparts

She would build a niche' come what may!

The loving parents doted on her

As she reached her age

To open the next page

The newly -weds, enchanted in their dream-world

Life blossomed and bloomed in fervor and zeal

Love, passion, desires filled the book of life

As it attenuated the pleasant, charming appeal

They doted on each other

As they reached their age

To open the next page

There were flowers and fragrance, sometimes a taste sour

They had a fulfilling life with children and more

The ups and downs of life, they faced holding hands

A life full of contentment like never before

They all doted on the family

As the children reached of age

And waited for their next page!

The beginning of the last rung of life awaits

A dawn of awakening, and realization as a sage

As they dote on the spiritual bliss they experience

They calmly and bravely wait for the next page!

38. Hard work: The key to success

Sweat it out!
The ladder of success has many rungs
Each needs to be climbed one by one
There's no jumping or missing of any
Neither the ritual of climbing can you shun!
The meaning of success is different for each
It may be power, money, fame or a goal
To some it may be just meeting their two ends
Yet to others, it might be purification of their souls!
There's no short cut but a clearly set out path
To achieve and accomplish for reaching an aim
Sheer hard work! Just sweat it out, and you'll see
You get your share of both name and fame!
Never give up trying the hard way to get your objective
The first step may be a failure despite diligent determination
Sweat it out and try again; keep trying
Success is got through inspiration and perspiration
To me, the means amounts more, than the end
The road taken towards success needs more significance
The arduous path of truth, honesty and ethics surely lead to success
Success should be measured as the beautiful journey – not the
consequence!

39. The road taken

Arduous wavy difficult paths as they were met
Many hurdles crossed as unachievable benchmarks set
Every route posed questions of integrity and values moral
Luring enticements and temptations that shook standards ideal
It wasn't easy, not succumbing to attractions on the way
Escaping from snares of greed which could lead me astray
Many wars were fought as the soul stood bare
Lessons of pragmatism and practicality into my eyes stared
Reasons and justifications for righteousness argued and sought
Instances of blossoming falsehood while internal battles were fought
My goals were set and intentions crystal clear
From cobwebs of pretense and fabrication I dared to steer
I earned peace and a conscience that couldn't be shaken
As l walk on road of righteousness that I've taken

40. Poetry in prose

The poetry stands in splendor, opulent in imagery and sheen

There's rhythm and rhyme, subtle innuendos sublime

Built as a royal castle, it glitters in princely pristine

Cascading from minds and hearts are pearls of wisdom

Markers of sensitivity and sound, with depth enormously profound,

Disciplined to toe the rules laid by the poetic kingdom

Poetry is bejeweled to bring forth some mystic spate

The special rhyming décor, giving away prose some succor

The ennui of the prose won over with verses ornate

Oh, poet! keep those enchanting verses alive in you

Let volleys of words dull, may not in your essence dwell

Every prose be ornamented with poems of varied hue

41. Greed

Unlimited and undesired longing
Even when there is no need
Hoarding of food for oneself
When there are starving mouths to feed
Material possessions pile up
Collections every limit exceed
Letting no one get anything
Their roads of access impede
In a competition to secure oneself
Virtues and conscience bleed
Unscroupulous means often play
Trampling on poor and helpless they succeed
No ethics, values or morality rules
Oh avarice ! thy name is greed !

42. Wish

I can see a beautiful tomorrow.
Where there would be only joys and no sorrow!
The skies would become the seraphic vault blue.
An arched rainbow vivid with motley hue!
The breeze would hum a cheerful melody
The leaves would rustle with a happy rhapsody!
The dark black clouds of dread and fear.
Would above the horizon of melancholy disappear!
Chirping birds would wipe away the gloom.
Welcoming each new day with greenery and blooms!
Laughter in every corner of the world resound.
With gaiety excitement and enchantment around!
Every breath of air ambrosial nectar pure.
The oceans and waters cerulean and azure!
Yes! there would again be sunny days in a trice
When our emotions of ecstasy and hope would rise!

43. Grand-mom's tales

Her tales brimmed with goodness
And spirit of cheer at home
There were elfs and angels dwarfs ,pixies and lucky gnomes
The princes rode horses
And stole the heart of beautiful lasses
The kings held durbars in courts
Or pronounce rules for the masses
From springs and streams pure water flowed
There was no thief there was no rogue
Every one had deeds like gold
Virtues and high morals was in vogue
Oh granny why did you lie?
And painted an idyllic mirth
Im hassled, harassed,pestered and piqued
As I search for humanity on this earth.

44. Deepawali

The lights shine, glitter, dazzle in the gleaming eyes
Crackers burst to create a smoky cloud in the skies
Beautiful colorful murals aesthetically adorning the floor
Variegated gateways or 'Torans' hanging on the door
Aroma of freshly made sweets in ghee pervades the air
Goddess Lakshmi uplifts every gloomy soul in despair
The light of knowledge shines, to darkness of ignorance dispel
Creating goodwill while dark desires and thoughts forever quell

45. Shades of love

Prayers in reverence with an emotional connect
Hands raised in veneration asking for inner peace
Unfathomable immense unconditional bonding
A mother's love for her children can never cease
Beloveds get attracted, infatuated, yearning for closeness
Wishing eons of togetherness for years many
Friends and buddies share and care for each other
Ever ready to take perilous plunges too many
Teachers imparting knowledge, their students love
Wishing they ascend and soar up the high skies
The mighty show love to the downtrodden
Wrapped in a selfish motive to fame and recognition rise
Oh love! your shades are varied and speckled in amazing hues
There are scary variations in subtle shades of gray
Wearing garbs of envy and possessiveness turning fatal
Love begets love, life but can breed hatred in a few.

46. Poetry from the soul

Poetry is the unexpected utterance of the soul
Scathing, condescending, disdainful darts
Attacked the crevices of the innocent heart
It bled in sorrowful bouts and poured
While the soul silently, ceaselessly, endured
Helplessly watching, with silent lips, in vain
The strings of sorrow fell as ink, to release pain
Every word spelt the feeble, vulnerability peaking
When lips are sealed, expressions do the speaking
The ink that flowed was unprecedented and uncontrolled
As it was bathed in a barrage of injuries to the soul.

47. Waiting for spring

Frosty winters freezing the crevices of the heart
Chilling the spine and fogging the brain
Misty mornings with dark silhouettes of the trees
The old aches and moans cringe in pain again
The swallows and the sparrows in hibernation hide
The cuckoo migrates to another bird's nest
The daffodils and the pink primroses disappear
The hustle bustle and merriment are put to rest
The chilly winters have ceased the flowing life
Oh, spring when would you appear? and frozen-hearts thaw
Usher in your fragrance in the blooms and blossoms
Let every injury heal unscarred, and no wounds remain raw
Let the colorful, varied and beautiful colors of spring
Ring in joyful ecstasy, welcoming a plethora of happiness wild
Chirping birds, fluttering feathers, aromatic ambience in clear skies
Make my essence go in rapturous glee like a child.

48. Save the girl child

Holding on to the umbilical cord tight
I saw a faint peeping light
I rushed to a corner to snuggle
Scrambling in the womb as I huddled
The lurking danger made me shiver in fear
Eluding, evading was too much to bear
My brazen killers stood with weapons and arms
As I failed to impress them with girlie charms
"Another girl? No way" my granny growled
To confirm my presence there was an army on prowl
Sobbing and crying, my mother wept aloud
My life was endangered in a wicked cloud
"Get rid of her "echoed all, including my dad
"Our legacy's bastion would be held only by a lad"
I begged, teary eyed, to let me, life breathe
But they were determined to bestow me a wreath
The doctor proved to be my savior fond and caring
She stood up for me as a shield daring
Quoting legalities and ethics she put them to silence
Refusing to harm me she rebuked them for the violence
If ever you dare to harm the girl child before she's born
Punishments and even prison would make your dusks and dawn!
I breathed a fresh whiff of fragrant air in style and stride
And continued my journey with dignity and pride

A girl is a Blessing to this universe' creation
Save the girl child *-should be every human being's mission.*

49. Fun of Holi

When clouds of colors scatter in vibrant ecstasy
The misty, powdery splendor in gay abandon wander
Drenched in pure emotion filling up to the brim
Hugging to embrace thirsty souls that meander
Water balloons and color filled pumps cascade
Spurting emotions of exuberant happiness and glee
The parched and arid hearts rejuvenate in joy
Shedding all the feelings of dread, despair or melancholy
Lip smacking sweets with a small dash of naughtiness
Everyone in a warm cuddle to bury hatred of the past
The air resonates with the mellifluous 'phaag' and the 'dhol'
Every heart beating to the rhythm to make the festivities last
The festival of colors announces the triumph of goodness
Spreading warmth and resonating love in every core
Fun-filled gaiety excitedly pulsates in all souls
Happiness prevails as every heart goodwill pours

50. The tumult within

An emotional turmoil, a whirlwind grasps you
When feelings lie dormant bottled within
Let them out as a spurt in a cascade
Free, liberated, like a free bird uncaged, to spin
Feelings lie scattered, hidden in crevices of the heart
They need to be expressed and outside thrown
Wounds need to heal, and leave no scar
Brewing them inside, would scald your soul own
Joys and feelings of happiness rejuvenate
Spreading cheer and gaiety to every spirited core
Empty the old cask full of dark gloom and despair
Let only love, warmth and beatitude overflow and pour

51. Colors of people

With twinkling smiles and goodness emanating
Spreading effervescence of virtuous rectitude
They assured the downtrodden amidst cheering crowds
As folded hands, teary eyes n heads bowed down in gratitude
The powerful and the mighty reverted to their self
As emptiness shrouded and all were gone
The poor were humiliated and disparaged again
Left in the lurch into abandonment and forlorn
The childhood friend who borrowed from me
Study materials that led her to the ladder of success
Upon meeting, had an air of vanity and pride
Suddenly putting on a mask of pretense and ignorance
The rich kinfolk looked down upon their own
When times were unpropitious and adversities struck
These same relatives then held in high esteem
When unfavorable times were overturned by luck
Oh people! how you change colors
Masked you remain as you live for years and more
Colors of convenience, colors of ease
Pretense, hypocrisy and feigning makes your core.

52. Quote poem 1

"Poetry is a deal of joy and pain and wonder with a dash of the
dictionary"
Khalil Gibran
Poetry is a deal of joy pain and wonder
Words those emanate and express the emotions from within
Find their outlet as poetry enriched with finesse pristine
Expressions of mixed feelings which to come out yearn
Happiness and joys and sometimes wounded in pain
Poetry is a deal, which few can fathom and churn
Sometimes its a potion for catharsis in an urn
The words dressed up with a dash of embellished jewels
Dormant in abysses of abandonment where they dwell
When they see the light of the beautiful morn
Its a wonder how could even pain be adorned !
An assortment of sorrows and joys concealed
Poetry is magical as it carries the power to heal

53. The premature girl-child

The family reveled and rejoiced
As they waited for my arrival soon
My mom protected me from danger
And my dad would proudly swoon
Calendars were marked and dates were saved
As days, weeks and months passed by
It's going to be some more weeks to go
Till then inside let the naughty angel lie
But the boisterous me wanted to come out
And explore the mighty, rough, wild world
It was getting too tough for me to stay in
From morn to night, lying up curled
I decided to give everyone a surprise
On the eve of a cold, New Year Day
I kicked and bounced and broke the pail
And announced my arrival that very same day
My parents trembled in anxiety and fear
She's so tiny, and of hardly any weight
Oh doctors! Please push her back to her bed
For her arrival this isn't the time or state.
The family prayed hard and worshiped all gods
But I had made up my mind to escape
I came out as a new year gift on a cold morn
In a precarious condition and a sorry shape

I was kept wrapped in warmth and wool
Tubes and needles poked me everywhere
I reached home amidst love and overwhelming joy
after a few days of careful watch and care.
I promised to give up my naughtiness
And did everything to happiness give
I'm indebted to my loving parents forever
Shall spread joys around as long as I live!

54. The changing colours of the world

As the red lured me into passionate love
The black and the grey pulled me from within
The white warned me thats everyones not so clean
Even love has its shades of envious green
The blues got over me every day
The yellow then visited to give me hope anew
The purlple splendor with its royalness winked
Do you not wish to own regal colours a few?
I sat in despair not knowing what to choose
The colourful gaeity was misleading my way
Every colour was of dual attribute and accord
The same on both sides of the horizon lay
This world is a mirage, illusions galore
What seems to be colourful is actually grey
Colours fade off, true shades expressed
The happiness entailed leads into dismay

55. Penance

She was parched and dry, wounded and abandoned
By her own children who were blinded by wealth
They wanted more and more; greediness galore
Resorting to means full of wickedness and stealth
They broke her branches, to make their abode
Dirtied her bosom from which she fed so many
Vandalizing, capturing and crushing her essence
Standing upon the graves by terror and tyranny
Her children suffered in silence as she dropped a tear
Her helpless cries did not their souls stir
Ruthlessly their horrific, monstrous laughter swayed
She was deprived of her cornucopia of water and air
Mother earth resolved to save her other children dumb
She penanced and flooded the earth with copious tears
Earthquakes, tornados, tsunamis shook their conscience
Until the evil humans pledged to protect for many years

56. Shelter

The city was burning with the fire of the arsenal
Hither and thither the crowd went into a frenzy mad
Loud cries were lost in the din of the melee'
Scattered and strewn lay injured and slain bodies scantily clad
She scampered her way along empty silent desolate lanes
With her new-born close to her bosom as she fled
Tens of thousands were running amok to save their lives
Her heart raced; adrenalin surged, as roads were painted red
Suddenly an invisible hand whisked her, to a corner dark
She was blindfolded and gagged, silenced and helpless made
Bundled and pushed into an already idling vehicle which sped
She could just feel movement and hear shouting voices fade
The vehicle screeched to a halt after a while,
She saw herself amongst a crowd running helter-skelter
She was welcomed with warmth, affection and love
As they had brought her into the safe havens of a shelter
She was relieved to see her own creed and countrymen
All rescued from the war hit injured motherland
She was reassured and counseled to make her believe
That she was sheltered, protected and amongst safe hands.

57. Love

Fathomless and boundless
An emotion so deep
Spreading goodwill and happiness
In bundles, stacks and heaps
The bonding between the mother and child
Friends, relatives, siblings and family
Unconditional, pure and selfless a feel
Remains pure and blossoming for posterity
The romantic love that's fueled
Amidst passions and desires of yearning intense
The worldly attributes of sensual pleasures
Sets a maze irresistible, of dreams in life immense
The devotional love with the Supreme Being
Steps up the quotient of spiritual ecstasy divine
The attachment to materially mortal things abates
And towards the pass of seeking self, one inclines
Oh love! How many faces have you?
Which one is the ultimate and true?
This universe thrives on the feelings of joy
Cherished by all; created and nurtured by you.

58. It is your smile

When the balls of cotton meander in the sky
When a cool drizzle quenches the earth parched and dry
When the ball of fire rises up on a cold winter day
Giving a surprise to children who want to play
When the breeze swooshes past, holding all in a trance
The tall trees sway to its rhythm and dance
The splash in the puddle as it misty droplets sprays
There occurs an aura of joy in the drudgery of the days
Blossoms and blooms fill the air with fragrance
Chirping feather friends twitter and sing in reverence
The heavenly orb carries the twinkling stars in its embrace
The silvery moon shines atop with princely grace
Gleeful happiness and pure bliss create an aura magical
Oh life! it's your smile that makes this creation so beautiful!

59. Poetry is the orphan of silence

Silence is not abstract, it does make some sound
Deprived of languages, it makes the experiences resound
Horrific stories or pleasant encounters, from nucleus come alive
Poetry gives it form and shape, nourishing it to survive
Silence had not spoken but gave words a voice
Life shared its periods of joy, helping all to rejoice
Words got from events, poetry tries to tell its tale
Leaving footprints in the sand of life, endeavoring to regale
There are two worlds, which through poetry, communicate
A connect is formed between the living and the inanimate
Poetry is the orphan of silence, yet breaths to life
The screaming tyranny of scathing sorrow, despair or strife.

60. Exam fever

The racing heart beats and sweaty palms
Futile attempts to remain calm
Last minute revisions and cramming
The syllabus is still uncovered and alarming
Sleeplessness becomes a daily guest
Every day of life is put to test
Food gulped and appetite lost
Time has to be overpowered at all costs
Books and notes scattered all over the study table
Praying that everything studied is from the brain retrievable
That awful feeling of under the weather
To face the monster all the courage gathered
Dressing sense lost and uneven pairs worn
Sometimes crumpled,unkempt or even torn
Lucky charms of varied types seen
A single nail painted in black or green
These days of emotional stress and worry
Oh God please blow off the flurry !

61. Unanswered questions

Why do we die and not live forever?
Why do innocents get slain?
Why goodness doesn't beget goodness
Why is there so much grief and pain?
Where does life come from and go
Where does the Sun and the moon set?
Why is there success for the undeserving?
While the hard workers nothing get?
Why don't the perpetrators get punished?
Why doesn't karma boomerang for all?
Why the unscrupulous rise up the stairs?
And the honest face a disgraceful fall?
What's past birth and its significances?
Which to every event we helplessly attribute?
Why can't we control time and travel on it?
And hold the circumstances to get to its root?
There is a myriad of questions which unanswered remain
No man on earth knows the solutions to any
Life is but mysterious, enigmatic, mystical a journey
While we wait for that impossible moment of epiphany!

62. The last page of my diary

Hundreds and thousands of pages from my life's diary
Created an affair of happiness and joyous glee
There were crests and troughs which pinnacled and plummetted
Yet were handled with adeptness and alacrity
Tears which dried leaving the eyes stony
Started flowing as the ink of erudite sensibility
The paths were arduous yet not immposible
As I tread on them with utmost responsibility
The inner voice crumbled and crashed like a coward
When it couldnt raise its voice against any atrocity
With a proud sense of fulfilment and contentment I look ahead
As my wrinkled hands scratch my deteriorating memory
I add more pages and won't let the last be last
As I hold the mantle of future for my progeny
Sometimes the ends
have only beginings
Which blossom into new buds for posterity

The last page of my diary

63. The Poet

Terrified and stupefied he translates
His suffering into words
Which he has weaved into an ornate, colorful embellishment
He pours his tears on paper, which as ink flow
Screaming to the world that he has been wronged
He shares his happiness with the words which he pens
Creating them from zilch as a wizard
The words do wonders, healing and curing
Others who suffered in silence
The poet has been blessed to mitigate pain
His words do magic and embrace
Crying hearts and souls which are forlorn
He and his reader both meet at the culmination
Of his verses that flow like a cascading stream
Both reach bliss as words of the poet are cathartic.

64. Life !you are my destiny

Tumultous and arduous roads of life
I travelled to carve my destiny
There were ripples of gloom;
blossoms and bloom
As I traversed those terrains with glee
With wings of passion I rode on winds
Flying high on clouds of wonderment
I ran the race,keeping up the pace
Climbing up the ladder from the ground to the crescent
Oh life's leaves! on a twisted twig !
You have given me my share of my nemesis I deserve
There are joyful smiles, or turbulent riles
I humbly accept your ruling with vigour and verve.
Destiny ! you are my beloved fate
I surrender to you, as you for me await
Bouquets and brickbats; slurs or affectionate pats
I embrace you with all fondness of a mate

65. Balance

Life should be balanced
Say they
All work and no play?
Eat a balanced diet for health
And why join the rat race for wealth?
Homemakers' balance with "me time" need to dare
Working women while should balance with family care
Children to balance their curriculum with sports should know
Senior citizens should balance by letting go
Husbands need to balance both at work and home- the boss
Wives need to balance their spendings with no loss!
Grooms need to balance their search for girl's fair
Brides need to balance their femininity with air
If you want your lives to be full of glee
Keeping it balanced and simple is the key.

66. Slipping sand

Those valuable footprints on the sand of life
Indelible, memorable etched on my mind
Those are epochs, benchmarking my destiny
Alas! If only I could travel back to catch up with time
Precious hours full of pride, they smirked as they passed
Time and tide wait for none don't you know?
I had moved to a context of a new zone of life
Regretting yet helplessly watching it go
Turning every moment to a past to look back upon!

67. The falling flowers

Adorned and ornate, perched atop
The fragrant flower bloomed with pride
It swayed and swaggered with aplomb
Conceited and vain, its arrogance it couldn't hide
The orchards were permeated with scent
As the blossoms swelled to tease the leaves
Hey! you dull green and yellow! push aside
Your colorless ordinary life is my only peeve
The yellow old leaf, to its petiole precariously clung
Gasping, it said "I was young and beautiful too yesterday"
Though I'd love to stay young and immortal
To the upcoming new posterity, I need to give way
The next day, the flower witnessed on her, a wither
Her swollen pride had drowned, as she looked weak
She was shattered as she hung from her weak stem,
Was she too destined to fall from the peak?
The yellow leaf hugged her tight in protection
Wrapped her gently in his weak embrace
I'll hold you as together we descend to fall down
In mortality lies nature's succor and solace!

The falling flowers

• 75 •

68. A lyrical leaf

The leaf of life, a lyrical, musical song
Melodies of happiness as you sing along
Harmonies and symphonies of the chord strings
A whiff of ebullient sunshine loads of ecstasy brings
The octaves run to new sonatas make mellifluous
As drops of honey laden words bring out energy copious
Beyond the horizon, the rhythm reverberates
The valleys of the heart chime and rejuvenate
The joys and sorrows that like music strike a balance
The waves of rhythms with crescendo and cadence
The leaf of life as it walks its musical sojourn
Spreading harmony till a new leaf is born.

69. Those were the days

Frolic and fun, where fairytales were spun
Carefree days of cheer, roads easy to steer
Happiness filling days, with none to run the rat race
Sunshine filling the lives, vibrant and colorful vibes
Hearts close to each other, camaraderie like brothers
Blossoms of flowers wild, fragrance in the essence smiled
Greenery across the earth, of foliage no dearth
The drizzly drops of rain, washing off the dreary mundane
Boisterous laughter of the child, exploring the raw and wild
The swim in the slushy waters, cries of naughty laughter
The horizon a clear sky, as the humming larks flew by
The universe as a blessing divine, every creation with the Supreme align
Life a harmonious melody with the hearts singing in rhythmic symphony
Chirpy feather friends to awaken tweet, the breezy morns an extravagant
feat
Those were the days of the yore, those with ecstatic bliss to the core
Now though mired in these days to earn, to live in those days aching
hearts yearn.

70. The paradox of desire

The evil elf of desirous and fascinating temptations
Leading to a path of woes, sorrow and destruction
Arising from the heart which, to satiate never ceases
The web spins around as yearning for pleasure increases
The never ending want for success and wealth
The plethora of wrongdoing to acquire by secrecy and stealth
It doesn't end here but cascades into a demon
Soon snowballing into a brute beastly villain
Paths of peace and tranquil if needs to be got
Limiting cravings and temptations in life needs be taught
Flames of passion and desire have to be soon doused
It's a volcano, with a whirl of repeated cravings housed
That would burn one's own soul if not restrained
The afflictions would be deep, entrenched in pain
The "desire to end the desire" should reign
So that in peace and harmony is the universe sustained

71. Broken

There were whispers and murmurs and soft undertones
She found herself accused as she stood shivering alone
Her attire, her demeanor, her gender was under fire
She had travelled in the night and fueled his desire
Why couldn't she cover herself and not show her skin fair?
Had she been confined to home, could any have dared?
She shouldn't have ventured out at this hour of night
It's she and only she responsible for her pitiful plight
A girl is a fire of passion and the boys cotton bales
Together they create havoc which cannot be blamed on males
Its upon the females to protect their bodies and souls
And not to create an uproar, a ruckus and later cry foul
She trembled first with fear which changed into rage
"If there is a wild beast let loose, its he who is to be caged
I'm not brittle or shattered and shall not let the day go unspoken
I will shout and nudge every girl till everyone's silence is broken!

72. Quote poem 2

A poem is a record of a discovery
Ted Kooser

I went to the lofty mountains and valleys deep
Watching the skies with the balls of wandering cloud
Ecstatic and liberated my sprits high soared
To the ethereal starry azure, my pneuma bowed
I discovered- I was a miniscule in the gigantic creation
Powerless and helpless in the mighty lap divine
My pride, ego and arrogance evaporated in the air
My conscience and my essence with the heavens intertwined
As I sat down to pen my buoyant feelings of joy
My words became the angelic witness of my verse
I had discovered my inner self in this bountiful world
Recording my overjoyed tryst with the enigmatic universe.

73. When you'll come back

Papa! I wont be naughty any more
And help mom in all her chores
I'd study and submit my homework in time
And would set my time-table with the clock's chime
The book shelf is now tidy and properly set
Every book,every article is now easy to get
I'd take my food and milk and no tantrums show
Am keeping my footwear in the shoe-rack in a row
I have kept all my gadgets and distractions aside
All your naggings now reverberate to me as a guide
Tis tough without you while youre fighting a war
Fresh wounds may heal only to leave deep scars
Papa! When you'll come back, you'll see a new me
I vow never to hurt you ; changes you'd visibly see
I'm waiting in eagerness hiding my stubborn tears
Papa! come back soon to treasure together many more years.

74. Time machine

I travelled to the past
And saw happiness last
Everyone was contented
There were joys that never ended
I saw greenery all around
There was chiming and chirpy sounds
Doors were open to one and all
Ethics, values and virtues stood tall
Needs were very little and few
Laughter ushered in mornings new
Brotherhood and camaraderie reigned
With one's agony others were pained
I now travelled to the future on the beast
There was doom and despair to say the least
Time travel taught me values of the yore
Let's not repeat those mistakes any more.

75. Environment dystopia

The air and despair
There wouldn't be any air
left to breathe
Air in bottles and banks would sell
One would be compelled to cough and cringe
Gasping and waiting to leave this living hell
Trees? oh, what are they? children would ask
There wouldn't be leaves in breeze to sway
Birds would tumble and fall dead from dry twigs
Hunger leading to snatch flesh from others every day
Tsunamis strike, as people rush to lives save
Meteoroids flash, acid rains and solar flares
Earth is now not friendly to human beings
With absent hair and lashes as they scare
Mass exodus in search of another abode
Where people trample, kick and kill without remorse
The poisonous smoky air turns children blue
Everything is just finished; no more unlimited resources
Summers chill and freeze while winters have downpours
Lakes freeze and then suddenly ice breaks to leak
There is nothing to eat or drink to survive
Existence on this planet now looks too bleak.

76. Thorn

It pricked, as it hid under the beautiful petals pink
My finger was bleeding, as it lay concealed
The flowers spread fragrance and hues of red
The bristles which hurt weren't revealed
Perfumed air whistled past bleeding souls
Tears wished to come out but lay concealed
Weepy eyes drank back the salty water
Pretentious laughter and smiles, the body revealed
Every beautiful rose has a hidden thorn
Yet the bruises on its petals lie concealed
Roses blush the very hands those crush it
The sadness that they harbor is never revealed.

LALITA VAITHEESWARAN

Thorn

77. The emotional rollercoaster

Happiness and joy looked past the road of life
There were peals of laughter with a fervor of glee
Ebullient exuberance of joyous merriment ruled
Buoyant spirits kept the aura bright and chirpy
There was a strange dark corner unlit and dark
With terrifying shivers down the spine, in crept fear
But erupted an angelic figure with an aura serene
I was taken aback with surprise as she drew near
She was a destitute stranded in isolation
She moved me to tears as she her story narrate
Her family had abandoned her as she developed a disease
Leaving her to suffer and meet a dying fate
Anger and disgust stung me as I my teeth ground
How can a family so cruelly disown its own part?
Let's all pledge to be there for one another
And spread love till death do us part.

78. A moment of happiness

Life is a rigmarole, braided in moments of frenzy
Some giving agony, others joyous ecstasy
Mornings of sunshine and evenings of dismay
Creating ripples of tumultuous emotional array
Clouds of uncertainty looming over arid souls yearning to swoon
A blanket of azure with stars and the angelic moon
Rains of tears that flood the valley of a bleeding heart
A breeze of unfaltering hope that nothing would fall apart
Drizzling moments of delight of rising after a fall
Jubilation and triumph of embracing in brotherhood all
Is happiness just a fleeting moment short-lived and transient?
Shouldn't we all strive to make it everlasting and permanent?
Each moment of life is a gift for eternal celebration
Rejoice every breath, pulse and rhythm in exultation
Happiness shouldn't be for 'a moment' but for eternity remain
Springing and oozing from our inner selves let happiness reign

79. The mystical cosmos

The golden rays of the miraculous, benevolent sun

Reflects its dazzling, cheerful, sunshine on everyone

Luminescent radiance, plays hide n seek with dusk, at eventide

Wandering, vagrant, white clouds in gay abandon float and glide

The azure, cerulean sky, with its vibrant, vast expanse afar

Holds dear in its bosom, the enigmatic, twinkling stars

The hallowed magical moon, with seraphic smiles ganders

Her milky magnificent ambrosia, dripping down on earth meanders

Blissfully hugging n tugging my esse, is the aromatic breeze

Merry making are shadowy, swaying, silhouettes of trees

Dancing to the melodious, mellifluous, symphony of the night

Whistling jocularly, a tune of ecstatic, euphoric rhapsody in delight

Cloaking and swaddling the smiling crescent, secretly whisking it away

Thunder rumbles and roars, painting those white cotton balls grey

Cuddling n huddling, whispering, embracing in glee as they hover

A drizzle begins its journey to metamorphose into a shower

A giant downpour overpowers to become a torrent to flow

Washing the earth of its dust ceasing the scorching woes

Drenching myself struck with awe, with bewilderment I look

The pitter- patter cleanses my soul; inundating as a brook

The reverberating petrichor into me, vitality and vigour permeate

Oh! enchanting nature! a magic, ethereal, surreal, mystical, you create!

This poem was awarded by the Asian Literary society in the annual

wordsmith contest 2021 and has been published in their anthology

80. The journey alone

Arduous terrains often challenge my way
From a straight path, dragging me astray
Luring and enticing me with bribes to silent remain
Threatening me with dire consequences to see me being slain
I have so many enemies who strangle and ensnare
I have to prove my existence, with courage, grit and dare
A cavalry of supporters my hand hold till midway
Foot sores, pain and agony do unbearably stay
Helplessly they give way to the thin straw of trust
Leaving me to struggle and fight back to falsehood bust
I'm tired and fatigued, having no one by my side
It's a lonely journey difficult, and a choppy ride
*I'm **TRUTH** and am on a journey alone*
The territories are grueling and my paths unknown!

81. The new dawn

Shackled to heavy metallic fetters n chains,
Of narrow-minded patriarchal outlook that disdains
Trembling, staggering, she rose from the ground,
Staring helplessly into the glaring, blinding light, spellbound
Knocking upon her gloomy, miserable, dingy dawn of despair
As she woke up to a new morn, her lips in a weak, silent prayer
She found a gift wrapped in ornate ribbons blue, red and green
sparkling as dew gems and sequins of motley hue, pristine
Beautiful flowers and blossoms spreading surreal aroma,
Tenderly hugged and tugged her wounded, yearning pneuma
With bated breath, she opened the package in delightful glee,
Clanking her chains. struggling in vain, to set herself free
Out came a tiny bottle with a magical potion of liberation,
Assuring and promising the prisoners of gifted emancipation
There was a decorated placard which had cautious advice and direction
The potion had to be consumed with courage, grit and determination
Self-reliance, education, showing courage to Saying NO to violence,
Confronting injustice fearlessly, and giving a voice to every silence
Get up! you have the power to change this regressive world legacy
Be the change, stand liberated, carrying the bastion of supremacy!
This poem was selected and has been published by the Asian Literary
society in their anthology 2021

82. No one knows my pain

Everything looks flowery, life spectacularly ornate
A plush opulent abode, and a handsome mate
Chaperones and maids, to cater to every sundry need
Varied tasty delicacies, satiating every gluttony greed
Full of chivalrous etiquette, well-dressed folks
Eloquently skillful, well-mannered, white collared blokes
Everything is perfect, by word of the dictionary list
But there's emptiness in me, even in everyone's amidst
I'm lonely and shrouded by pensiveness immense
Dominated by patriarchal egomaniacs' un-remorseful arrogance
Prideful egotism to degrade and attack where my dignity dwells
Closed lips and tears arrested to tell others "all's well"
No one knows my pain; I'm on my journey alone
The gloom, the misery and desolation is but my own!

83. Clouds

Roaming in gay abandon, like children, at play
I see balls of cotton meandering away
Somersaulting their way, to span the skies wide
Suddenly darkening the daylight, as the golden ball, they hide
Squealing in joy, from their grip, the sun they set free
Only to gather together as a giant cloak in symphony
Playing hide and seek with the silvery stars and moon
Pausing to peep and guffaw at arid souls and swoon
Clouds hover in starlit nights as if in a search
Changing colors like a naughty chameleon, they on heavens perch
They're impatient and angry as they loudly rumble
On a patch of famine, droughty earth they inadvertently stumble
Quenching the thirsts of terrains, they drop, pour, and drizzle
Melting and drenching parting hearts in love, after the barren sizzle

Clouds

84. The missing anklet

The anklet had bells which chimed and pealed
As the pretty lass proudly flaunted her bauble
It was made of gold and had beads of red stone
It shone and gleamed on the pretty and fair ankle
She hopped and danced with the ornament in joy
Oblivious to the surrounding miseries and gloom
Her world was bejeweled, speckled and hued
While she rejoiced in the spectacular bloom
Suddenly the clang and the peal subdued
To her amazement only one anklet shone
The other foot looked unembellished and bare
A hunt began for the ornament lone
Aghast and inconsolable, she wept aloud
Sure, that she had been robbed by her maid
She called the cops to apprehend the simpleton
And every trap to detain her she laid
The maid was arrested amid her pleas of innocence
Her cries ran into the girl's deaf ears, alas!
The next day, as she hopped and danced again
She treaded on the missing anklet lying on the grass

85. Joyful reverie

I'm gleeful, joyful; the universe smiles with me
Vibrant is the world,
As happiness unfolds
A beautiful creation for everyone to see
There's a spirit of festivity all around
My feet spring up to dance
My heart ready to romance
Every creature on earth making me spellbound
There's blissful rapture and ecstasy
My fears all gone
Insecurities I have none
The blooms are on a blossoming spree

86. Confusion

Entangled emotions, disheveled sentiments

Unclear, uncertainty clouding the mind

Why is it not as simple as it appears to be?

Complex knotty cobwebs intricately intertwined

Unanswered questions prodding inquisitive curiosity

Dismal darkness making pessimistic conclusions

Racing hearts and pounding beats echoing gloom

Even the setting sun portrays dreary illusions

Just close your eyes and calm incensed passions

Let the mind be intelligible and crystal clear

Unravel and disentangle shreds one by one

Widen your horizon to broaden your sphere

Set aside all worries, braving them as they come

Let pre-conceived notions have no place near

Tackle courageously with calmness serene

Valiantly allaying the monster of fear

87. Behind the wall

She came as a newly-wed with the customary fanfare
Entering the room with the anklets' chime and tinkle
As laughter permeated the aura around
She tried her best with strangers to mingle
As dusk made its way to empty darkness of the night
She awoke shivering to cries of helplessness from around
Trying to overhear, broken noises from behind the wall
She was trying hard to decipher the eerie sounds
Suddenly she was gently pushed and rebuked for her prying ears
"You are the new bride so be subservient and coy", said they
With pounding heart, ashen and timorous with shudder, she looked
Curiousness gotten over her; there was unquestionably a foul play
Not the giving up kind, she soon the authorities summoned
The wall was broken, uncanny was the pathetic sight
Another bride was shackled, chained and secretively hidden
Secrets behind the wall were unearthed and brought to light

88. If we ever meet again

I would never be lured into shadows of delusion
Shunning your idyllic presence in ignorance
I'd protect you and preserve you for posterity
Never denying your precious existence
I'd hold you in gentle, enfolding caress
Breathing your fragrance and ambrosia divine
Nothing in this life would ever replace you
I have realized with rues that only you were mine
If only you could hear my cries in pain
Voices in wilderness echoing from afar and yonder
My life is a void with silent rhythms and beats
Aimlessly hither and thither it meanders and wanders
Oh, days of the yore! I tearfully feel your absence
Can't we have a tete-a- tete yet again once more?
The flowers and the blooms and the carefree sky
Rejoicing and basking in love like ne'er before.

89. Wisdom

Wisdom and knowledge walked hand in hand
Knowledge proudly said that he was in command
Wisdom was shy as she had nothing to brag
She was carrying only her experiences in her bag
As it was getting dark, roads became vague and dim
Knowledge had his road-map which could beat the grim
Both cautiously walked on a precarious narrow lane
Wisdom was skeptical about unknown perils in the terrain
Her astute reasoning came to her rescue in time
She stopped abruptly just short of an explosive mine
Knowledge accepted that there's much more and beyond
Presence of mind in action is what simply wisdom donned
Old adages and proverbs have within them engrained right
In every word, a galaxy of enlightenment and insight
An in-depth understanding of each nuance to the core
Wisdom is humble that it knows no more!

90. Tears of misery

A feeling of melancholy, gloom and despair
Reigned on her as her eyes swelled up with tears
Homeless, abandoned, penniless, she roamed
She had lost all her nears and dears
Crestfallen and forlorn she was wandering
At least one known soul would be alive
The war had alas ruined one and all
She was the only one to survive
Heavy-hearted she cried in pain and woe
Oh! Heavens why didn't you devour me too?
Despondent and depressed her eyes turned dry
In these ravaged ruins where do I go?

91. Solution for pollution

Your keys to good health rests with you!
So, protect and guard your environmental milieu
Keep the pollution under check
Else your body systems become a wreck
To junk foods, say a big no no
And let your body normally grow
Pesticides and pollutants in the air
Leave one infertile and in despair
Causing diseases of endocrine glands
On obesity and thyroid diseases, one does land
Chromosomal anomalies, and babies premature
Dangers and diseases which have no cure
Let's be part of the environmental solution
And pledge to reduce every pollution

Clean environ-Green environ

Invented verse forms

All verse forms were invented but there are forms which are different from the traditional ones, which have been inspiring many.

Some of these forms have being created and displayed here.

92. LANoe

When life throws at you only gloom
And you live in the fear of doom
Let hope bloom
The end of darkness brings bright light
Life then becomes a merry sight
Travel light
Throw out negative thoughts afar
Let life comprise peace and not war
Erase scars
Colorful spread of merry cheer
Life with its blissfulness is here
Have no fear

93. Pi Poem

Thunderous violet skies
Pour
Clasping every leaf tight
Clinging
Only to leave it again
Falling copiously on parched, dry, arid, thirsty, infertile land
Smiling earth
Emanates fragrant petrichor pervading the air
Sleeping seeds cheerfully shun dormancy
Hailing the rains!
Small leaflets adorned with silver
That shine like dew infusing life, vitality and energy
Farmers cheer in glee thanking the Heavens for benevolence
They had toiled hard for this day
Drizzling and pouring the Rain-Gods give them their living
No starving anymore!

94. Ecstasy(Huitain)

The birds chirped in the whistling breeze

while the trees made a rustling sound

A stream gurgled along to tease

Taking a wavy turn around

Happiness in nature was found

As ding dong chimed the temple bells

My spirit felt pure bliss profound

To unearth where ecstasy dwells

95. Mono-tetra rhymes

Red, violet, pink, mauve and blue
Motley flowers of diverse hue
The garden blossoms just as new
With sparkling dew, with sparkling dew

Swaying to the rich fragrant air
A sight, with delight, as I stare
The petals peals of laughter bear
Cosmic affair, cosmic affair

96. Karma(Tetractys)

It

Comes back

To catch you

Giving your due

Better to spread only goodness around

97. Autumn(Ronka)

As Autumn makes the leaves fall down
Taking leave from their abode so dear
Pays magical colorful tributes to the ground
Awed, sitting on the hills we stare
An enchanted season of souls is here!

98. Moonlight(Argonelles)

Milky

Celestial moonlight bright

Makes luminescence scattered lie

Seraphic smiles donning the sky

Brightens an inky night

Holy

An ambrosia divine

A shadowy misty glimmer

Paradise glitters to shimmer

With a radiant shine

99. Whitney Poem

Back bencher
Distracting all
Teacher irked
To front seat called
As he came
Sans any books
Was made to stand facing wall

100. Love(2,3,4,5 poem)

Your love
In my heart
Blossoms like red flowers
Never to wither and die!
My love
Blooms and grows
Showering petals of fragrance
Fueling passion to fly high!
Let love
Be so strong
Shackle our hearts together
till in peace we lie!

GLOSSARY

Glossary-lanoe

Invented by Lisa Ann Noe, lanoe has mono-rhymed tercets (3-line stanza) with an easy rhythm.

The elements of the LANoe are:

~stanzaic, written in no less than 3 tercets and no more than 8 tercets

~syllabic, L1 and L2 are 8 syllables each. L3 is 3 syllables.

~rhymed, rhyme scheme aaa bbb ccc ddd etc.

Pi Poem

The Pi is built up in words and follows the mathematical number that stands for Pi:

PI = 3.141592653589793

In lines:

line 1: 3 words

line 2: 1 word

line 3: 4 words

line 4: 1 word

line 5: 5 words

line 6: 9 words

line 7: 2 words

line 8: 6 words

line 9: 5 words

line 10: 3 words

line 11: 5 words

line 12: 8 words

line 13: 9 words

line 14: 7 words

line 15: 9 words

line 16: 3 words

The Huitain

The Huitain

- Is a French form
- Which as actually written as a verse of a primitive ballade in the 14th century.
- The first known author of the Huitain is Guillaume de Machaut.
- The early huitain had two rhymes in its rhyme scheme (ABABBAAB)
- One century later, the definitive form of the huitain was formed, and it contains eight lines, with eight syllables per line, and the rhyming scheme is ABABBCBC

The Mono-tetra

The monotetra is a poetic form developed by Michael Walker. Here are the basic rules:

Comprised of quatrains (four-line stanzas) in tetrameter (four metrical feet) for a total of 8 syllables per line

Each quatrain consists of mono-rhymed lines (so each line in the first stanza has the same type of rhyme, as does each line in the second stanza, etc.)

The final line of each stanza repeats the same four syllables

This poem can be as short as one quatrain and as long as a poet wishes

The Tetractys

The Tetractys contains five lines with a total of 20 syllables, divided as follows:

line 1 - 1 syllable

line 2 - 2 syllables

line 3 - 3 syllables

line 4 - 4 syllables

line 5 - 10 syllables

Ronka

The ronka is composed of 5 lines, each having 7 words without concern for syllables. No rhyme. An observation of the day, either inside, outside or internal.

Argonelles

- 5 line stanza
- Syllabic,syllable per line are 2-6-8-8-6
- Rhymed,rhyme schemes -xabba xcddc xeffe x being unrhymed

Whitney

This titled syllabic form, created by Betty Ann Whitney, has exactly seven lines.

Syllable Pattern: 3/4/3/4/3/4/7

2,3,4,5 Poem

A 2345 poem

Means

2 words in first line

3 words in second line and so on